NOAH'S TOWN
Adventures in Economic Development

MAURY FORMAN
Educator / Humorist

MILT PRIGGEE
Illustrator

INTRODUCTION

Cartoons and comics have been a part of my entire professional life. When I was in health care I used them to teach patient care to children and non-English speaking patients; started a company, Cartoon, Inc, that curated cartoon art shows for museums and libraries; wrote three cartoon history books, and created over 500 cartoons for my economic development blogs, books, and presentations.

Comic strips are excellent learning tools that often deal with real life issues. They allow people to see life from different viewpoints, raise awareness for current issues, inspire and even teach us what it means to be human. The images and limited text convey ideas that can be expressed with drama, puns, humor, and satire.

Not only do they amuse, but they provide human teachable moments where we may see ourselves. In the comic strip *Blondie*, Dagwood is an office manager in a construction company and his wife, Blondie is an entrepreneur who started a catering business—the first women-owned business in the comics. These fictional stories help us make sense of our own existence. No wonder so many comics adorn the cubicles and office refrigerators in countries around the world.

Crises can be both challenges and opportunities. They certainly are for the residents of Noah's Town. A crisis can spur innovation, and in these times, economic developers are looked upon as leaders of innovation to create sustainable communities and regions. Rural strategies, entrepreneurship, apprenticeships, remote working, and pop-up stores are all strategies that act as catalysts to rebuild society in new ways post-pandemic. *Noah's Town* addresses all these issues with humor and wisdom.

Noah's Town is just three panels of characters with stories told in about 40 words. Will you find it funny? I hope so. Will you learn something? Probably. Will you see the correlation between reality and imagination as practitioners in economic development? Definitely.

- Maury

1

5

21

44

61

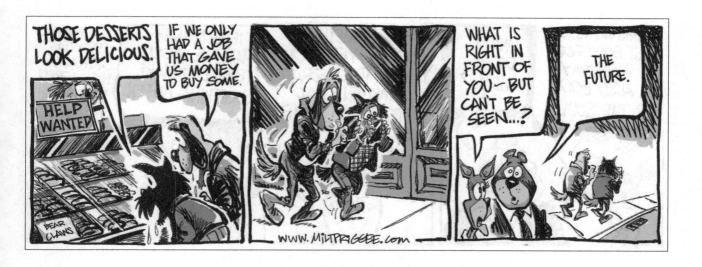

81

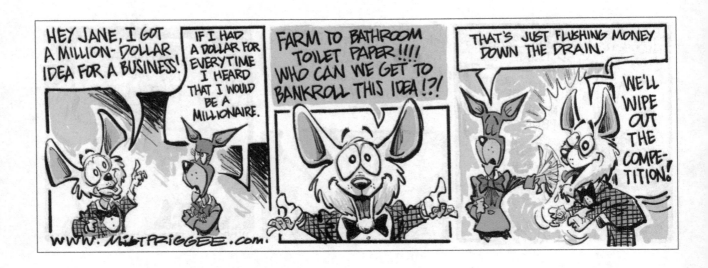

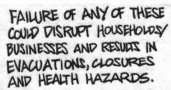

ACKNOWLEDGMENTS

Writing any kind of book is like economic development. It is a team activity. No economic developer will be successful without colleagues to bounce ideas off of and partners to implement those ideas. In other words, self-reliance takes a village.

I have been fortunate to have had great colleagues and partners in my 30 years as an educator and practitioner in economic development. To exclude their influence in getting this book out would be like an economic developer ignoring the small businesses and non-profit organizations that are the heartbeat of a community.

First, I would like to thank economic development organizations like WEDA and especially the IEDC who continue to produce conferences that share best practices and innovative and sustainable strategies to the practitioner. I am also beholden to the Washington State Department of Commerce, formerly known as DTED, CTED and TED for employing someone with no knowledge of economic development yet allowing him to teach with wit, wisdom and creativity.

I am also grateful to Udaya Patnaik, Robb Zerr and Gretchen Schlomann for their brainstorming, editing, and production of these strips. Their willingness to take my calls during all hours of the day or evening has allowed me to sleep well at night. I am indebted to Linda Alongi, my work partner, who made all of my crazy ideas and game show tools come to life. Without her, I would never have recognized my goal as a game show educator. To Karen McArthur for making sure that I not only had a budget to educate but also that everything I did was legal. To Dr. Jennifer Korfiatis, for not only keeping me supplied with soft in the middle chocolate chip cookies but also who taught me that "once a teacher, always a student". Her lifelong commitment to learning ignited my imagination to educate through humor.

This book would be just a bunch of words if I had not partnered with my talented friend Milt Priggee. His artwork brought *Noah's Town* to life and showed how a bunch of animals could escape disaster and become a sustainable community.

And finally to all the economic developers I have met and wondered if these comic strips in *Noah's Town* were inspired by them.

MAURY FORMAN was the Senior Manager for Rural Strategies with the Washington State Department of Commerce for 30 years where he focused on creating healthy communities and developing a culture of entrepreneurship in rural areas. He was the founder and director of the award-winning Northwest Economic Development course at Central Washington University that taught over 2500 students the skills and tools of an economic developer. He has delivered keynote presentations and technical assistance to thousands of practitioners across the U.S. and Canada. Maury has received leadership and lifetime achievement awards from the International Economic Development Council.

Combining wit and wisdom, Maury has written 22 books for the economic development profession. His previous book, *Noah's Town: Where Animals Reign,* is a 21st century fable about disaster preparation and recovery.

Maury's work can be found at: mauryforum.com

For the past half century **MILT PRIGGEE** has freelanced award-winning political cartoons, caricatures and illustrations for newspapers, magazines, books, websites, television, and radio stations.

He's worked for print platforms in Chicago, Ohio, Kansas, and Washington state. His political cartoons and a comic strip were nationally syndicated. Milt's political commentary has appeared in *The NY Times, Washington Post,* CNN, MSNBC and a number of refrigerators across America. He was the first cartoonist for *Crain's Chicago Business* and the last cartoonist for the *Puget Sound Business Journal.*

In 2000 he was awarded a journalism fellowship to the University of Michigan amongst his many other awards and served as president of the Association of American Editorial Cartoonists.

To see more of Milt's commentary and artwork go to: miltpriggee.com

ADDITIONAL BOOKS by MAURY FORMAN

Available on Amazon.com

Noah's Town: Where Animals Reign
A 21st century fable about disaster preparation and recovery.

The Wit and Wisdom of an Economic Developer
A compendium of blogs and original cartoons based on 30 years as an educator/practitioner.

Startup Wisdom: 27 Strategies for Raising Business Capital
Discover 27 non-traditional strategies for raising business capital.

Your Town: An Amazing Destination
Visit dozens of best practices that lead to 25 immutable rules of successful tourism.

Learning to Lead
The basic coursebook that identifies the most essential strategies for practitioners.

Journey to Jobs
Learn techniques of successful recruitment and retention from 14 site selectors and practitioners.

Community Wisdom 2
Practical and fun tips, ideas, and thoughts on a variety of subjects for community success.

Available as free download from Mauryforum.com

Washington Dollars, Washington Sense
A playbook for investors, businesses and communities for local investment.

10 Commandments of Community Leadership
10 commandments with 100 ideas for leaders to create vibrant and sustainable communities.

Made in the USA
Monee, IL
05 October 2024

67229515R10063